WONDER STARTERS

Cars

Pictures by CLAUDE KAILER
and ROSEMARY LOWNDES

Published by WONDER BOOKS
A Division of Grosset & Dunlap, Inc.
A NATIONAL GENERAL COMPANY
51 Madison Avenue   New York, N.Y. 10010

Published in the United States by Wonder Books, a Division of Grosset & Dunlap, Inc., a National General Company.

ISBN: 0-448-09668-4 (Trade Edition)
ISBN: 0-448-06388-3 (Library Edition)

FIRST PRINTING 1973

© Macdonald and Company (Publishers), Limited, 1971, London. All rights reserved.

Printed and bound in the United States.

Library of Congress Catalog Card Number: 73-1971

Our car has stopped.
A tire is flat.
Daddy must change the wheel.

Daddy puts the spare wheel on.
We put the other wheel in the trunk.

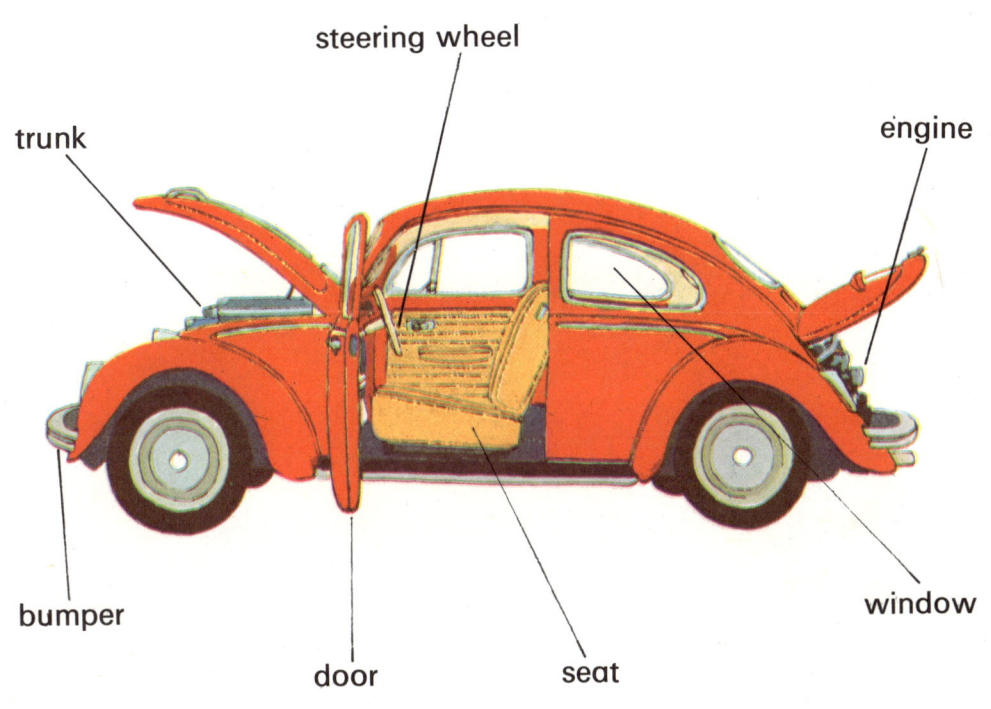

Our car is a German car.
The trunk is at the front.
The engine is at the back.

Cars are made in factories.
This factory makes 5,000 cars in one day.

A tractor-trailer takes cars to a ship.
The cars are put on the ship.

Ships take cars to many countries.

This is a car made in the United States.
Most of these cars are big.

This is an English car.
This English car is very small.

8

This is a French car.
It is on a bumpy road.

This is an Italian car.
It is a sports car.
Sports cars can go fast.
10

This is a racing car.
It has room for one man.

Racing cars go very fast.
One racing car has crashed.

This car has crashed on the road.
It went too fast.

This car skids on the wet road.
It has bad tires.

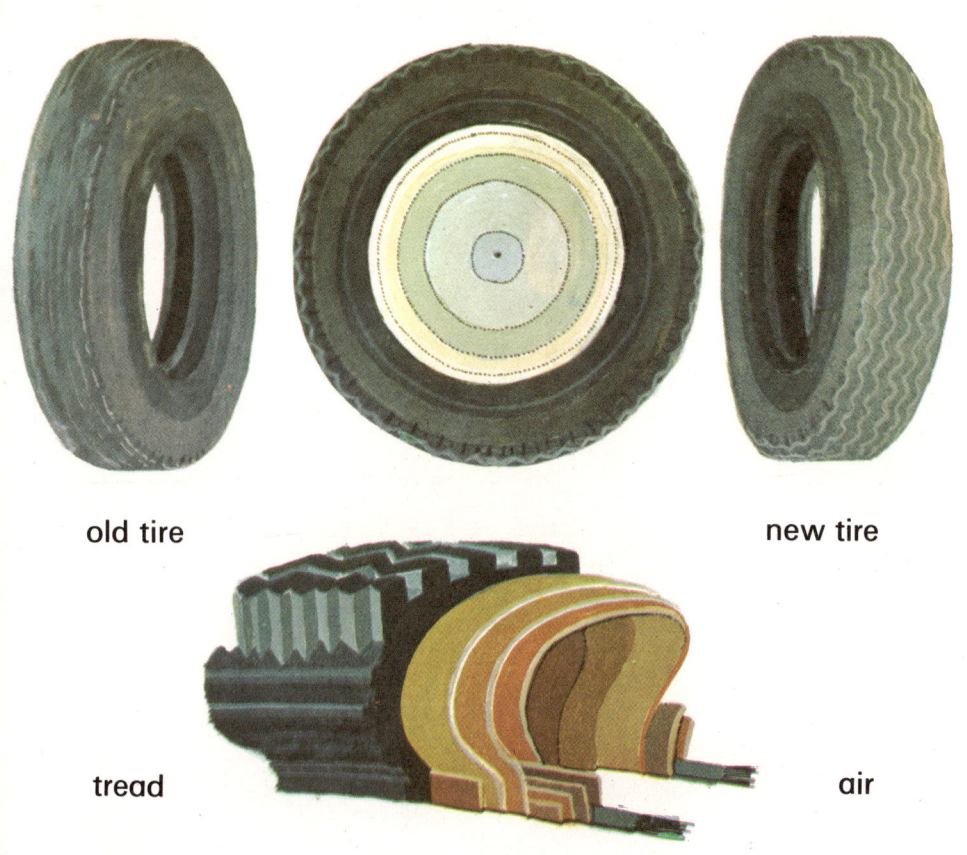

old tire

new tire

tread

air

Tires are made of rubber.
They are filled with air.

15

Here is a very old car.
It moved by steam.

This old car had two seats.

Here is another old car.
It carried four people.

Here is an old racing car.
It had a very big engine.

Here is a jet car.
Jet cars are the fastest cars.

See for yourself

Look for cars from different countries. How many of these cars can you see?

Here are some cars from other countries.

Starter's Cars words

wheel
(page 1)

flat tire
(page 1)

trunk
(page 3)

engine
(page 3)

factory
(page 4)

tractor-trailer
(page 5)

United States car
(page 7)

English car
(page 8)

23

French car
(page 9)

Italian car
(page 10)

racing car
(page 11)

crash
(page 13)

skid
(page 14)

steam
(page 16)

seat
(page 17)

jet car
(page 20)

24